Raising a family, we wanted to instill a prayer life into our children. One of the biggest obstacles was a recognition of our own prayer lives being lacking. In studying scripture, we have also noticed many modern Christians have a poor understanding of how to pray. Not only did we want to instill a habit of prayer in ourselves and in our children, but we also wanted to model "good" prayers for our children.

We stumbled upon a traditional Jewish prayer from the time of Jesus and began to dig. As we dug into the prayer, we discovered there are many prayers that early Christians from a Jewish heritage would have prayed at different times and in different situations. There is a lot of nuance to the timing and situations for the different types of prayers, and we did not want to get bogged down in the specifics of all the different types of prayers. But we did recognize that these prayers were extremely beautiful prayers and poems.

What we have compiled here is our take on that tradition. This is not exactly correct for the 1st-century customs but is how we have incorporated these prayers into our lives. We have also melded other prayer aspects into our customs, such as impromptu prayers or unscripted prayers. Sometimes we add in Psalms as well. This is simply a structure we follow and build off of.

We hope that as you use this book it helps focus you throughout the day on God's work and you find yourself rooted more deeply in Him. We hope that you are blessed and grow in prayer.

Prayers Throughout The Day

Modeh Ani – PRAYER UPON WAKING

I come before Your face, offering my gratitude, King, living and enduring,

Who returns my life afresh within me with nurturing love.

Your trustworthiness overflows!

The loyal love of the LORD is never finished, His nurturing love is never spent,

They are fresh each dawn. Your trustworthiness is abundant!

Lamentations 3:22-23

I am the LORD, and there is not another, apart from Me no God exists.
I make you succeed, though you do not see Me,

So that they may know, from the rising of the sun and to its setting place, that there
ceases to be anything without Me;
I am the LORD, and there is not another.

I squeeze light into shape and establish purpose for darkness, I work perfect peace
and establish purpose for bad, I am the Lord, I work all these things.

~Isaiah 45:5-7

Yotzer Ham'orot – BLESSING FOR THE MORNING

Blessed are You, LORD our God, King of all creation,
Who gives light its shape and darkness its purpose,
Who accomplishes peace and sets all things in order.
Blessed are You, LORD, the one who sculpts the lights!

Tefilla Yeshua – PRAYER AT NOONTIME

Our Father, among the heavens, set Your name apart from all other names. Come, bring Your authority as King and grow it throughout the nations. Make Your desires a reality here on the land in the same way they are in the heavens. Gift us with the bread we need each day. Cast away from us the consequences of our failures, as we also cast away the consequences of those who fail us. Do not lead us through places of testing. Nevertheless, snatch us away from any bad we face.

You then, whenever you pray, enter into your hiding place and close up the entrance. Then, pray to your Father who is concealed. Your Father, who perceives what is in concealment will recompense you.
~Matthew 6:6

Ma'ariv Aravim – Blessing for the Evening

Blessed are You, Lord our God, King of all creation,
Who, by His Word, blends the lights of evening.
God, living and enduring, may He continually reign over us
To the vanishing point and to the end.
Blessed are You, Lord, who blends the lights of evening!

Let my prayer be established as sacrificial smoke to Your face,
The raising up of my palms as the offering of the evening!
~Psalm 141:2

Bedtime Blessings

Blessed are You, Lord our God, King of all creation,
Who establishes order for daytime and nighttime.
He rolls away the daylight from the face of darkness,
And darkness from the face of the dawn.
Blessed are You, Lord, the One who blends the lights of evening!

Hear Israel, the Lord is our God, He is our only God.
Blessed be the Name of glory.
His kingdom is to the vanishing point and to the end.
Love the Lord your God with all of your heart,
With all of your soul, and with all of your strength.

Blessed are You, Lord our God, King of all creation,
Who causes the bands of sleep to fall upon my eyes
And deep slumber upon my eyelids.
May it be the delight of Your face,
Lord my God and the God of my fathers,
To let me lie down for the night in peace and safety
And to let me arise in the morning in peace and safety.
In Your hand You watch over my spirit.
You have loosed the cords that bound me,
Lord, the God we can trust!

God saw the light was good

And God distinguished between the light and between the darkness.

And God called the name belonging to the light "day"

And to the darkness He called the name "night".

And there was twilight and there was daybreak: the first day.

~Genesis 1:4-5

In the peace of my wholeness I will lie down and sleep,

For You, Lord, alone set me in security.

~Psalm 4:8

In Your hand You watch over my spirit;

You have loosed me, LORD, God of trustworthiness.

~Psalm 31:5

Hear, Israel, the LORD is our God, the LORD only. And you shall love the LORD your God with all of your heart and with all of your soul and with all of your strength. And these words which I have put in order for you today will be upon your heart. And you will sharpen them to your sons and will speak of them in your sitting within your house and in your going in the path and in your lying down and in your arising. And you will tie them as a reminder upon your hand and they will be as blinders between your eyes. And you will engrave them into the posts of your house and gates.

When your son asks you later on, saying, "What are these witnesses and wisdom teachings and justice practices which the LORD our God set in order to you?" then you will say to your son, "We were slaves to Pharaoh in Egypt and the LORD brought us out from Egypt with a hand of strength. The LORD gave demonstrations and conspicuous deeds, mighty and terrible, against Egypt, Pharaoh, and all his house in our sight. And He brought us out from there so He could bring us in to give us the land which He had promised to our fathers. And the LORD set in order for us to work all these wisdom teachings, to fear the LORD our God always, for our good, as it is today. And it will be righteousness to us if we are watchful to work all this commandment in the face of the LORD our God just as He set in order for us."

~Deuteronomy 6:4-9, 20-25

Prayers Surrounding Meals

She'ha'kol – General Blessing before Food and Drink

Blessed are You, Lord our God, King of all creation,
Who brings into being all things by His Word!

Our Lord and our God, You are deserving to carry the praise and the esteem and the power, because You made all things for life, and because of Your decree they exist and are habitable.
~Revelation 4:11

Birkat Ha'mazon – BLESSING AFTER A MEAL

Blessed are You, LORD our God,
King of all creation,
Who prepares a continual feast of His goodness
For all the ends of creation to grow fat upon
Because of His love,
Which is generous, loyal, and nurturing.

He gives bread to all flesh,
For His love is loyal to the very ends.

Through His mighty goodness,
Scarcity has never come upon us,
And we will not lack food
To the vanishing point and to the ends,
Out of the abundance of His great name.

For He is God, who nourishes and sustains all,
And does good to all,
And prepares food for all His creatures,
Which He has given purpose to.

Blessed are You, LORD,
The One who provides our bounty!

*The eyes of all hope in You
and You give to them their
food in their time. You open
wide Your hand and sate
every living thing's desire.
~Psalm 145:15-16*

Surrounding Bible (Torah) Study

La'asok B'divrei Torah – Blessing Before Bible (Torah) Study

Blessed are You, Lord our God, King of all creation,
Who has set us apart as His treasured possession
By revealing to us His wisdom
And has instructed us to continually meditate
On the words of His teaching!

And now, if you will completely listen to My voice and keep My covenant, then you will be a treasured possession to Me out of all the peoples, for all the land is Mine.
~Exodus 19:5

Master, after whom
would we follow?
Your words hold life
without end.
And we have trusted
and now see
that You are the One of
God's holiness.
~John 6:68-69

Natan Lanu Torat Emet – Blessing After Bible (Torah) Study

Blessed are You, Lord our God, King of all creation,
Who gives to us the trustworthy teaching
Of salvation through our Messiah,
And life to the vanishing point He has set among us.
Blessed are You, Lord, Giver of the Teaching!

Other Prayers

Derek Ha'Yeshuah – BLESSING FOR SALVATION

Blessed are You, LORD our God,
King of all creation,
Who gives to us the path of
Salvation in Messiah Jesus.
Truly, He is blessed!

*And there will be a highway and path.
And it will be called "The Way of
Holiness". Those not made clean will
not cross over it, but it will be for him
who walks in it's way. Even the foolish
will not err.*

~Isaiah 35:8

Batish'bakhot – PRAISING OUR KING

Blessed are You, LORD,
The King to be praised for all to hear!

Extend your hands to the LORD! Call out in His name! Make His exploits known in all the peoples! Sing to Him! Make music to Him! Bring forth all that distinguishes Him! Boast in the name of His holiness! Be glad, hearts of you who seek the LORD!

~1 Chronicles 16:8-10

He drew us out from
the tyranny of darkness, and
carried us away to the
dominion of His beloved
Son, before whom we have
rescue, the liberty from sins.

~Colossians 1:13-14

Yetzer Ha'ra – PRAYER FOR RESCUE
FROM BAD INTENTIONS

Blessed are You, LORD our God,
King of all creation.
Let it be pleasing before Your face,
LORD our God
And the God of our fathers,
That you would weave Your teaching
Into our souls,
And pursue us with Your wisdom.
Do not let us go
Into the hands of Sin,
Nor into the hands of
Transgression and crookedness,
Nor into the hands of
Testing and ridicule,
And do not let bad intentions
Hold dominion over us.

And the centurion responded, "Master, I am not sufficient that under my roof You come, nevertheless, only speak forth Your word and my servant will be made whole."
~Matthew 8:8

Refu'ah Shelemah – PRAYER FOR PERFECT HEALING

Mend us, LORD, and we will be healed;
Deliver us, and we will be set free.
For our boast is in You alone.
Lift up perfect restoration over all our ailments,
For, God, You rule over our health
With faithfulness and compassion.
Blessed are You, LORD, the Healer of Your sick people!

www.ingramcontent.com/pod-product-compliance
Lightning Source LLC
LaVergne TN
LVRC092209141224
798957LV00018B/371